Theme 1

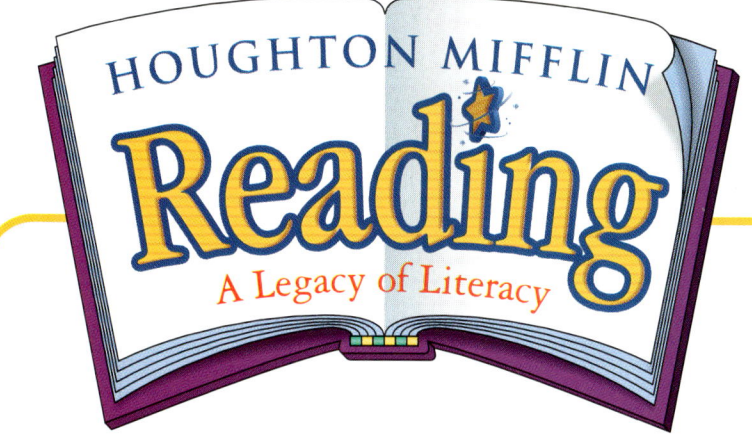

All Together Now

HOUGHTON MIFFLIN

BOSTON • MORRIS PLAINS, NJ

California • Colorado • Georgia • Illinois • New Jersey • Texas

Copyright © 2001 by Houghton Mifflin Company.
All rights reserved.

No part of this work may be reproduced or transmitted in any form or by any means, electronic or mechanical, including photocopying or recording, or by any information storage or retrieval system without the prior written permission of Houghton Mifflin Company unless such copying is expressly permitted by federal copyright law. Address inquiries to School Permissions, Houghton Mifflin Company, 222 Berkeley Street, Boston, MA 02116.

Printed in the U.S.A.

ISBN: 0-618-07492-9

3456789-BS-06 05 04 03 02 01 00

Design, Art Management, and Page Production: Studio Goodwin Sturges

Contents

Cat 5
Cat on the Mat 9
Cat Sat 13
Nan Cat 17
Fat Cat 21
Tan Fan 25
Can It Fit? 29
Who Can Hit? 33
One Big Fat Fig 37

Cat

by Jason Weeks
illustrated by Joan Paley

Cat

mat

Cat sat.

Cat sat, sat, sat.

Cat on the Mat

by Diane Patek
illustrated by Ora Eitan

Cat sat, sat, sat.

Cat sat, sat, sat.

Cat sat on the mat.

Cat sat, sat, sat.

Cat Sat

by Ruth Kwan
illustrated by René K. Moreno

Cat sat.

Cat sat.

Go, Cat!

Cat sat, sat, sat on the mat.

Nan Cat

by Kelly Teele
illustrated by Bari Weissman

Nat sat on the mat.

Nat can pat Nan Cat.

Nat can fan Nan Cat.

Go, Nan, go!

Fat Cat

by Sid Jones
illustrated by John Wallace

Nan sat here.

Pat, Nat, and Fan sat.

Fat Cat sat.

We can pat Fat Cat.

Tan Fan

by Randolph Silva
illustrated by Miki J. Yamamoto

We can pat Tan Fan.

Nat can pat Tan Fan, too.

Tan Fan can jump.

Nan can not pat Tan Fan.

Can It Fit?

by Lorraine Merrill
illustrated by Cathy McQuitty

Can the hat fit the pig?

Can it fit the rat?

Can it fit the bat?

It can fit the big cat!

Who Can Hit?

by Lisa Crane
illustrated by Andrea Arroyo

Have a big bat, Nan.

Nan can hit it to Nat.

Nan ran, ran, ran.

Nan can sit!

One Big Fat Fig

by Jason Weeks
illustrated by René K. Moreno

Pat can find a big fat fig.

Can Pat hit the big fig?

Pat ran. Pat hit the big fig.

Pat bit the big fat fig.

Word Lists

Theme 1, Week 1

Cat (p. 5) accompanies *The Cat Sat* and *The Mat*.

Decodable Words
New
Consonants *c, m, s, t:* *Cat, mat, sat*
Words with *-at:* *Cat, mat, sat*

Theme 1, Week 1

Cat on the Mat (p. 9) accompanies *The Cat Sat* and *The Mat*.

Decodable Words
New
Consonants *c, m, s, t:* *Cat, mat, sat*
Words with *-at:* *Cat, mat, sat*

High-Frequency Words
New
on, the

Theme 1, Week 1

Cat Sat (p. 13) accompanies *The Cat Sat* and *The Mat*.

Decodable Words
New
Consonants *c, m, s, t:* *Cat, mat, sat*
Words with *-at:* *Cat, mat, sat*

High-Frequency Words
New
go, on, the

Theme 1, Week 2
Nan Cat (p. 17) accompanies *Nan and Fan* and *We Can!*

Decodable Words
New
Consonants *f, n, p:* can, fan, Nan, Nat, pat
Words with *-an:* can, fan, Nan
Previously Taught
Cat, mat, sat

High-Frequency Words
Previously Taught
go, on, the

Theme 1, Week 2
Fat Cat (p. 21) accompanies *Nan and Fan* and *We Can!*

Decodable Words
New
Consonants *f, n, p:* can, Fan, Fat, Nan, Nat, Pat
Words with *-an:* can, Fan, Nan
Previously Taught
Cat, sat

High-Frequency Words
New
and, here, we

Theme 1, Week 2

Tan Fan (p. 25) accompanies *Nan and Fan* and *We Can!*

Decodable Words
New
Consonants *f, n, p:* can, Fan, Nan, Nat, pat, Tan
Words with *-an:* can, Fan, Nan, Tan

High-Frequency Words
New
jump, not, too, we

Theme 1, Week 3

Can It Fit? (p. 29) accompanies *The Big Hit* and *Big Pig*.

Decodable Words
New
Consonants *b, g, h, r:* bat, big, hat, pig, rat
Words with *-ig, -it:* big, pig, fit, it

Previously Taught
can, cat

High-Frequency Words
Previously Taught
the

Theme 1, Week 3

Who Can Hit? (p. 33) accompanies *The Big Hit* and *Big Pig*.

Decodable Words
New
Consonants *b, g, h, r:* bat, big, hit, ran
Words with *-ig, -it:* big, hit, it, sit
Previously Taught
can, Nan, Nat

High-Frequency Words
New
a, have, to, who

Theme 1, Week 3

One Big Fat Fig (p. 37) accompanies *The Big Hit* and *Big Pig*.

Decodable Words
New
Consonants *b, g, h, r:* big, bit, fig, hit, ran
Words with *-ig, -it:* big, fig, bit, hit
Previously Taught
can, fat, Pat

High-Frequency Words
New
a, find, one
Previously Taught
the